**BASED ON AMERICAN
DESCENDANTS OF SLAVERY**

# INTRODUCTION TO INDIGENOUS URBAN GARDENING

I0418216

## WRITTEN BY DAKU AKAWU

Published by Lee's Press and Publishing Company
www.LeesPress.net

Lee's PRESS | *A Premiere Self-Publishing Services Company*

ISBN-13: 979-8-9860989-5-1

*Paperback*

# Table of Contents

# Foreword

The great twentieth-century historian, Dr. John Henrik Clarke, reminded us of the importance of agriculture as it relates to community survival and responsibility. Other leaders have reminded us that if the ruling class won't treat you right, then certainly we can't expect them to teach you right. As an urban gardener, I would add that surely, we can't expect them to feed us right either. We often complain that urban and suburban areas are lacking in healthy food options. Obesity, high blood pressure, diabetes, heart disease, and a plethora of diet-related illnesses and diseases should be all the evidence we need to distrust, or at the very least question the source of our food supply.

Many vegans, vegetarians, and so-called health experts will tell you that changing your diet is the absolute solution to these health issues. What few will tell you is that the source of the meat imported into urban and suburban areas is more likely than not the same source of many of your fruits and vegetables. It's quite obvious that we must make dietary lifestyle changes if we want to decrease our chances of becoming ill or acquiring these food-borne diseases.

Over the years, I've interviewed many elders in the so-called Native American and African American communities. The generational knowledge they shared with me spans over one hundred years. One of the reoccurring themes in their stories was about how their families were able to survive on virtually no money and no health care. The so-called great depression in America lasted approximately twelve years. At the height of the American great depression, the unemployment rate rose to twenty-five percent. By the second year of the depression, food riots began breaking out across the United States.

The great depression in America was merely a continuation of the African American great depression which continues to this day. The end of the American great depression marked the beginning of the great exodus of African Americans from the southeastern United States. The great exodus was the second migration of African Americans from the southeastern United States. During the first migration, one and a half million black people left the south and headed west and north. The first migration ended after the start of the American great depression. Survival reasons made it more feasible to hold on to the land than to move to western and northern urban areas. Typically, city dwellers depend on others to provide them with food. So, moving to the city tends to force people to be dependent on others for all or most of their daily needs including food.

During the thirty years of the great exodus (also known as the second great migration) five million black people left the southeastern states seeking to escape domestic terrorism. They were also seeking economic freedom. What they seemed to forget was that land is the basis for the freedom they were seeking. While many of us live in urban and suburban areas today, quite a few of the homes in which we live sit on small plots of land that can be used for various purposes including growing food.

One of our most influential leaders has called for us to donate money so that we can buy farmland on which to produce food for our own community. There's no doubt in my mind that this is a noble cause in which to invest. That being said, since we are still in the midst of a great depression, it would behoove us to take inventory of the land we already have at our disposal and repurpose much of that land to grow food for ourselves.

My hope is that this book will help you change your perspective on farming/gardening.

# Plant Spacing

When we think of farming, we tend to visualize acres and acres of rows and rows of the same fruits and vegetables. If this is what we envision, obviously we will need to change our approach in order to farm in a small-spaced urban or suburban setting.

First, we have to determine exactly how much space we have to dedicate to growing food. Some may feel the space they have is too small and thus a waste of time. It's really just a matter of understanding how to utilize the space you have.

Many homeowners have at least ten by ten feet of yard space. That's one hundred and twenty square feet of land. Using forty square feet for access paths or walkways will leave each on average eighty square feet of land. It doesn't sound like a lot of space, but this is ample land to grow food. Some plants require more space, and some require less space to grow. Keeping this in mind, you will need to determine how much space you'll be willing to sacrifice for each plant.

A single bush tomato plant may require four square feet of space. If you decide to grow four, you will be sacrificing sixteen square feet. This will decrease your garden space significantly, but if you really like tomatoes, it may be worth the sacrifice.

While you will need sixteen square feet of space to grow four bush tomato plants, you can grow 32 collard green plants or one hundred and forty-four spinach plants in the same amount of space. It depends on what you want to grow and what you can grow in your environment.

# Sunlight

Sunlight is a primary factor when growing food. While leafy greens can grow in partial shade, fruiting plants require significant sunlight to grow to their full potential.

Before planting seeds, you must be aware of how much sunlight exposure your garden space receives daily. If the plant you want to grow requires at least seven hours of sunlight and your garden only receives a maximum of five hours of sunlight, you may need to decide to plant something more suitable to your environment.

Some parts of your garden may receive more sunlight than other parts. You will need to observe your yard to determine if this is the case. If your front yard receives more sun, plant sun-loving plants in the front yard. Perhaps you get more shade in the front yard. In this case, plant the shade-loving plants in the front yard.

# The Planting Seasons

Another thing to consider is the season. Some plants grow better in cooler temperatures, and some grow better in warmer temperatures. Tomatoes grow best in the summer. Collard greens grow best in the fall. If you're thinking that there are a lot of things to consider while urban farming or gardening, you're right. Don't let this discourage you though. Once you understand the basics, you will be well on your way to gardening success.

The time it takes to grow a plant from seed to harvest varies depending on the plant. While radish takes four weeks, bush beans take eight weeks, okra takes twelve weeks, and peppers take nineteen weeks. If you want to grow strawberries, be prepared to wait three years for them to bear fruit. Asparagus is another plant that takes three years to harvest.

The growing season also varies depending on where you live. If you live in New York City, your summer growing season will be shorter than someone that lives in Jacksonville Florida. This will affect what you will be able to grow and when you will need to plant your seeds. Florida would be a more ideal place to grow oranges, and New York would be more suitable for growing kale. This doesn't mean that it would be impossible to grow food suitable for another area on your land, but you may need to make adaptations to help your plants survive.

# Gardening Adaptations

Building a greenhouse in which to grow your food may be one such adaptation. In a greenhouse, you can extend the growing season by controlling the temperature, adding artificial lighting, controlling the humidity, etc. The adaptations can be very expensive and might put undue financial strain on people going through an economic depression. I have built many greenhouses using sturdy and inexpensive building materials that were accumulated over time.

There is so much you can do with cinder blocks using the temporary building techniques of many of our ancestors. The same cinder blocks used to build your summer raised garden beds can be converted into mini greenhouse garden structures. I have been able to keep my tomato plant cuttings alive in my temporary unheated greenhouse through December when nighttime temperatures can dip into the twenties.

Building your greenhouse in a sunny location is of utmost importance if you won't be using artificial heating or lighting. I built my unheated mini greenhouses in an area that only gets four to six hours of sunlight in the winter. This is great for growing leafy green vegetables but not ideal for fruiting plants. To grow fruiting plants successfully, you will more likely than not have to add artificial heat and grow lights to your greenhouse. If money is not an issue for you, it might be worth investing in a heated greenhouse especially if you want year-round fruit and you happen to live in cities like Boston, Chicago, or Detroit.

# Plant Nutrients

Like humans, plants need nutrients to grow and stay healthy during their lifespan. Having a basic understanding of how plants feed and what they feed on will help you grow healthy plants. There are essential nutrients that are basically food for plants.

A plant cannot grow to full maturity unless it has access to a sufficient supply of each essential nutrient element. Three of these nutrient elements are obtained from the atmosphere: hydrogen, carbon, and oxygen. The other nutrient elements are obtained from the soil. These nutrients can be broken down into three groups. The first group is the primary macronutrient elements which include nitrogen, phosphorus, and potassium. The next group is the secondary macronutrient elements which include sulfur, magnesium, and calcium. The third group is the micronutrients which include iron, boron, manganese, zinc, molybdenum, and copper.

Despite what the average gardener may believe, nutrients can be added to the soil without depleting your savings. By observing and emulating nature's processes, you can build your own nutrient-dense soil. Of course, until you gain the knowledge needed to build your own healthy soil, there are many organic soils you can purchase at your local hardware store or plant nursery.

Purchasing soils and soil amendments can be costly, but it may be necessary to do so until you develop the knowledge to make your own.

Don't waste your time trying to grow plants in unhealthy or

infertile soil. If you observe what you may consider weeds and grass growing in your yard, it may be a clue that you have fertile soil (at least topsoil).

It's also important to determine the depth of your fertile soil as some plants have deeper roots than others. Lettuce for example has shallow roots and can be grown in eight inches of soil. Bush tomatoes on the other hand typically need at least two feet of soil depth in which to grow.

As important as fertile land is for growing food, it's not absolutely necessary.

# Container Gardening

The most popular urban food production practice just may be container gardening. There are many upsides to container gardening. The thing I like most about container gardening is the portability of the containers.

One year I had my containers in an area that got plenty of sun in early spring, but by early summer, the same area was shaded by the leaf growth of several trees. Because I used containers, I was able to move the plants to a sunnier area of the property. The best growing medium for containers is potting mix, not garden soil. Homemade potting mix recipes are available free online, or you can always purchase pre-made organic potting mix which is available at your average local hardware store or plant nursery.

Containers are available in many different styles and sizes. They can be purchased or made from recycled and repurposed materials. Containers are made of various materials such as clay, resin, plastic, wood, etcetera. I prefer clay and wood containers for my outdoor plants, but I'm not averse to using well-made food-grade plastic.

Try to avoid cheap plastic dollar store containers as they tend to break easily, and reportedly, the plastic used to make them may be toxic.

In addition to growing food in containers, I have used large containers successfully as compost bins. To do this, simply fill the bottom third of your container with old or new potting mix, add worms, and add raw organic (oil-free) plant-based kitchen scraps daily. Also, add tree leaves, untreated grass clippings, and other literally green yard material as they become available.

I have inadvertently grown eggplant and ginger in my compost container. The most fertile potting mix remains in my compost container after three years of composting. My compost containers are always left in my garden. You can cover the containers with a breathable material such as a weed barrier or fencing to help keep animals out while allowing air and moisture in.

# Garden "Pests" & Beneficial Insects

I should mention that my gardens are located in Washington D.C., so there isn't a great deal of wildlife with which to be concerned. I've had to contend primarily with groundhogs and the occasional deer. While insects and animals may be considered garden pests, they are just part of our ecosystem.

Our ancestors lived in harmony with the natural world around them. As much as we have changed the natural habitat of our insect and animal neighbors, they still live among us. Either we can figure out how to live with them in harmony or we can continue the practice of slaughtering every large, small, and microscopic animal in our gardens.

Fencing is a very good deterrent for large and small animals but controlling insects can be a bigger challenge. A popular pest control method is using a floating row cover that lets the sun, air, and rain in and keeps small animals and insects out. Floating row covers may be found at your local hardware store, plant nursery, or online.

Nature is equipped with many checks and balances. In a healthy environment, unwanted insects are controlled by other insects. In the world of gardening, these insects are referred to as beneficial insects.

Almost certainly, plant-damaging insects will arrive in your garden, but how do you attract beneficial insects to your garden? Over the years, I have observed that plants provide us with everything we need to survive. Clothes, shelter, food, tools, paint, and even many weapons all come from plant material. Because every action has a counteraction, plants that attract unwanted insects should be planted among plants that attract insects that prey on your unwanted visitors.

When I was a novice gardener, I used to say, "If I can't eat it, I won't grow it." As I gained more knowledge and experience, I began to realize that every plant has its purpose. Flowers, I thought, only served the purpose of beautification. I was totally wrong about that. Planting all types of colorful flowers throughout your garden will attract a variety of beneficial insects. Besides that, fact, some flowers are also edible. Who knew?

Another way to deal with unwanted insects is to plant insect-repelling herbs and spices throughout your garden. Some of these insect-repelling plants specialize in less than a few insects. Lemon balm and lemon thyme, for example, both specialize in repelling mosquitoes. Other plants repel a host of insects. Catnip, for example, repels aphids, squash bugs, flea beetles, potato beetles, cabbage loopers, and more. Another example is dill. They repel aphids, squash bugs, spider mites, cabbage loopers, and white flies. Some insect-repelling plants such as peppermint and spearmint are invasive and should be kept in containers, or they will take over your garden. Do not plant them directly in the soil, or insects will be the least of your worries.

As our pre-colonial ancestors taught us, everything in nature serves a purpose. So, avoid the western practice of killing everything in sight.

# Beneficial Weeds

Believe it or not, weeds even serve a purpose in your garden. As a result of colonization, we have forgotten the purpose of many of these weeds. We are still aware, however, of certain weeds that serve a positive purpose in our gardens. Dandelion root is not only beneficial for human health, but it also aerates the soil and enables the plants to accumulate nutrients which are left in the soil when the plant dies. Dandelion roots will absorb everything in the soil including pesticides and herbicides, so do not ingest dandelion that has been exposed to poisons in the ground.

Other weeds that benefit your garden are ground ivy, chickweed, nettles, and clover. While you may want to prevent these weeds from taking over your garden, they should at the same time be encouraged to grow under your (or the gardener's) control of course.

While many gardeners are accustomed to purchasing chemical fertilizers, beneficial weeds can fertilize your soil for free. If you are fortunate to have fertile soil in your urban garden, try not to add chemicals of any kind. If you do add chemicals, give nature time to purge itself of these unwanted poisons.

Living in urban and densely populated suburban areas limits our ability to control toxins in the soil. If neighbors use chemical fertilizers, herbicides, and pesticides, the runoff can leak into your garden.

Moorish-raised Garden beds (much like containers) help isolate garden plants from these toxins by literally raising the garden above ground level. The higher the garden beds can be raised above ground level the greater the protection from toxins put into the soil by neighbors.

Much of my urban garden is raised two to three feet above ground level. This is because most of my neighbors practice genocide of everything on their property except grass. So the biggest pests you may have to deal with are your urban and suburban neighbors.

## Watering

As a side note, a raised bed helps people with disabilities, seniors, or others that have difficulty stooping or bending get access to the garden.

The deeper/larger your container or raised bed, the less you may have to water. In my three-foot-deep containers, I only watered them when it didn't rain significantly in over a week. I only use tap water when I have depleted my harvested rainwater.

I collect my rainwater in any sterile containers I can get my hands on. The size of the containers in which I collect the rain varies. I've used containers as small as eight-ounce water bottles and as large as a fifty-five-gallon garbage can. You can also purchase rain barrels to connect to the downspouts of your home.

The roof of your home or building is an excellent "catcher's mitt" for rain. After harvesting rain, it's important to put an air-tight lid or covering on the containers. If you don't, mosquitoes will lay their eggs in the water, and you'll have a mosquito infestation to deal with in no time.

Self-watering containers are a great way to limit the frequency in which you will have to water the plants, but mosquitoes can find their way into the water reservoir and lay their eggs there.

Another way to limit manual watering is to use drip irrigation, but fellow gardeners that use this technique have told me that their water bills increased significantly. I don't use drip irrigation myself, but I only mention it here to make you aware of your options.

Keep in mind that most typical garden vegetables do not like to sit in water. It's important to ensure proper drainage for your plants. Water your plants at the base of the plant in the morning; be careful not to water the leaves or fruit if possible.

Some plants like mint, thyme, and oregano don't need to be watered frequently once they are well established. Other plants like tomatoes need to be watered once every two or three days (more if they're growing in containers).

# Obtaining Plants

All this talk about gardening and we haven't mentioned where to acquire your plants. If you haven't noticed yet, I advocate spending as little money as possible while gardening. While it may be easier to purchase seedlings, it's much more expensive than growing plants from seed or growing from cuttings. Seedlings in my area are generally two dollars or more. Comparatively, you can grow dozens of seedlings from seed for that price. Buying seeds is relatively inexpensive but harvesting seeds from plants you've already grown is absolutely free.

If you're going to harvest your seeds, ensure they are completely dry. Once dry, store them in an airtight container such as a sealed sandwich bag, sealed envelope, paper bag, mini mason jar, etc. Make sure you label your harvested seed containers, so you'll know what you're planting.

There are two basic ways to grow plants from seeds. One way is to germinate the seeds indoors, and then when they are mature enough, transplant the seedlings into the garden. Some plants don't transplant well, so it would be better to plant the seeds directly in the garden as weather conditions permit. Many gardeners refer to this method as "direct sowing." You could also sow the seeds in the containers in which they'll grow from seed to harvest. This can take up a lot of space in your indoor "germination station" (as I like to call it), so this method may not be practical.

While growing plants from seeds can cost a little money and buying seedlings can be quite expensive, growing plants from cuttings can be absolutely free.

I'll share how to grow plants from cuttings in an urban garden book as this book is just an introduction to urban gardening.

It's important to understand when to plant your seasonal veggies. If you haven't noticed by now, two of my favorite garden plants are tomatoes and collard greens.

As mentioned earlier, tomatoes are grown primarily in the summer months and can take up to five months to go from seed to harvest. If you live in an area with four seasons, each season is typically only three months in duration. In this case, you can start growing your tomato plants indoors as early as mid-March (late winter).

After the plants have been growing indoors for two months, you can usually move them outdoors. By mid-July, you may have harvest-ready tomatoes.

Collard green seeds can be planted indoors in early March. By early May, the seedlings can be planted in the garden, and they will be harvest-ready by late May. The best time to plant collard seeds directly in the garden is early August. By late October, the collards will be harvest-ready. Collards planted in August can be harvested throughout the winter.

Cucumbers generally only take two months to grow from seed to harvest. If you desire harvest-ready cucumbers in mid-July, the seeds can be planted directly in the garden in mid-May.

Other plants like beets can grow in multiple seasons. Beet seeds can be planted directly in the garden as early as mid-April and take two months to grow to maturity. Beet seeds can be grown in the spring, summer, and fall.

While beets can be grown in three seasons, lettuce can be grown in all four seasons. Lettuce seeds can be planted directly in the garden as early as the first week in April (in the D.C. area). They can be planted indoors as early as the first week in March. Lettuce can be grown in partial shade during the summer months. When planted in the fall, they can be grown and harvested through the winter.

# Plant With Multiple Plant Parts

As we talk about harvesting plants, it's important to point out that many have more than one edible part. While we typically eat beetroot, the leaves are also edible. The commonly eaten parts of broccoli are the stems and flowers, but the leaves are also edible. It's well known that the onion bulb as well as the leaves are edible, but did you know that sweet potato leaves are also edible? Most people eat parsley tops, but parsley roots are also edible. Squash fruit is commonly eaten but its flowers are also edible. Watermelon fruit is typically eaten but its seeds and rind are also edible. When you think about it, you'll realize that the ability to feed ourselves is not just a dream but a realistic and easily attainable goal.

Even if the masses won't join the movement of indigenous and so-called "minority" people to feed the community, it can and is being done on an individual basis throughout this country and the world.

# Closing

There is so much information we can share on urban gardening such as crop rotation or even guerrilla gardening, but the goal of this book was simply to provide you with a brief introduction to the topic.

It is my goal to continue bringing you urban and suburban gardening information and practical guidance from a primarily low-income and indigenous or "minority" perspective. As I like to say, "If each one can reach one, and each one can teach one, certainly each one can feed one. If each one of us can feed one of us, none of us will go hungry."